Art Media

Written by Kay Ward, Ian Miller and Kirsty McLean

Published by World Teachers Press®

MW00568325

Published with the permission of R.I.C. Publications Pty. Ltd.

Copyright © 1999 by Didax, Inc., Rowley, MA 01969. All rights reserved.

First published by R.I.C. Publications Pty. Ltd., Perth, Western Australia.

Limited reproduction permission: The publisher grants permission to individual teachers who have purchased this book to reproduce the blackline masters as needed for use with their own students. Reproduction for an entire school or school district or for commercial use is prohibited.

Printed in the United States of America.

Order Number 2-5087
ISBN 1-58324-009-8

A B C D E F 99 00 01 02

Didax
Educational Resources

395 Main Street
Rowley, MA 01969

Foreword

Art Media is designed for teachers needing to teach their students art, but wanting to do more than drawing and coloring. The beauty of this book is that you don't need to be an art teacher to do the activities. The step-by-step, uncomplicated instructions allow anyone to produce impressive results, and have fun at the same time! The skill pages can be enlarged and used as a classroom resource; while the hint pages supply handy background information and tips on making the lesson run as smoothly as possible. Extension and research activities are also provided. The areas covered in *Art Media* are: construction, clay, painting, fabric and fiber, and print making.

Contents

Construction – Teachers Notes

Construction differs from flat media because:
- it has volume;
- its shape defines the three-dimensional space it occupies;
- it has many different viewpoints and is not seen just in profile; and
- it can be seen from different angles, directions, and distances under different light conditions.

Hints

- Use a variety of shapes and sizes.

- Use color to transform surface appearance.

- Add texture such as twigs, twine, dried leaves and buttons.

- Use decorative features (e.g. curled paper and color on tin foil) to enhance the surface of the object.

- Include movement to change the shape of your object (e.g. mobiles, kites).

- Alter the appearance of the materials you use so they are not easily identifiable (e.g. cut corners off boxes, pierce surfaces, tear, crumple, braid, lace, unravel, weave, wrinkle, crimp, knot, hang, outline, fold, slot, paint, texture, collage, score, or curl).

Extension and Research

- Create a temporary 3-D sculpture using materials available in the nearest vicinity of the completed work, e.g. river bank, beach, woods, or road side.

- Produce a 3-D sculpture using wooden poles as a basic framework. Other materials may be incorporated to add interest to the viewer. Hang free-moving modules within the main structure.

- Using rolled paper, construct a 3-D sculpture of a:

  - fantasy fish;

  - aggressive alligator;

  - giant funny bunny;

  - mythological beast;

  - big baby bird; or an

  - incredible car.

 World Teachers Press® Resource Book

Construction – Skills

6 When cutting paper, turn the paper, not the scissors.

@ Use construction paper or any heavy paper substitute to make any basic shapes. Experiment to make a piece of paper stand up and/or support other appendages.

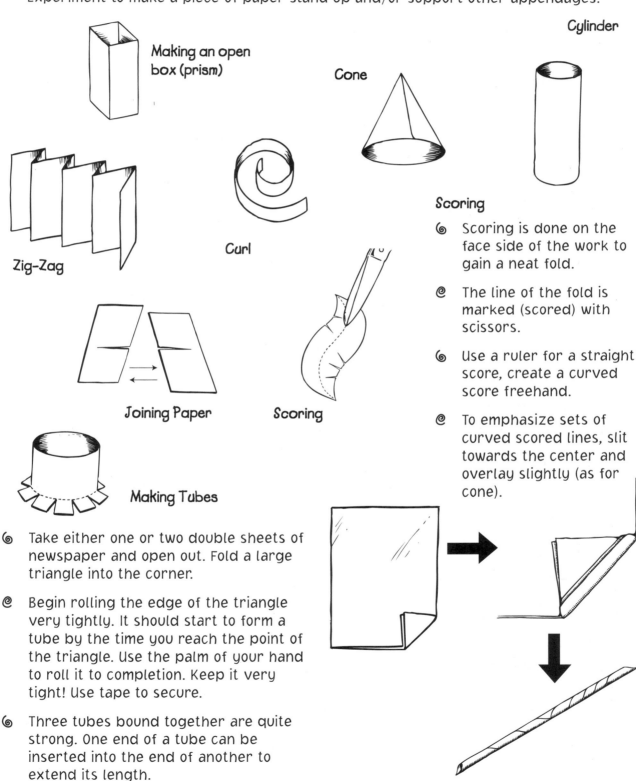

Making an open box (prism)

Cone

Cylinder

Zig-Zag

Curl

Joining Paper

Scoring

Making Tubes

Scoring

6 Scoring is done on the face side of the work to gain a neat fold.

@ The line of the fold is marked (scored) with scissors.

6 Use a ruler for a straight score, create a curved score freehand.

@ To emphasize sets of curved scored lines, slit towards the center and overlay slightly (as for cone).

6 Take either one or two double sheets of newspaper and open out. Fold a large triangle into the corner.

@ Begin rolling the edge of the triangle very tightly. It should start to form a tube by the time you reach the point of the triangle. Use the palm of your hand to roll it to completion. Keep it very tight! Use tape to secure.

6 Three tubes bound together are quite strong. One end of a tube can be inserted into the end of another to extend its length.

Construction – Skills (Extension)

Extending Paper Usage (continued from page 5)

(continued from page 5)

- ✆ Combine paper types/colors.

- ✆ Repetition is very important.

- ✆ Variation also needed, e.g. same decoration, different colors...

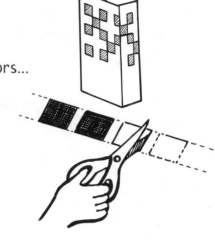

Surface Treatment Ideas

- ✆ Cut into surface area when flat with a craft knife to let in light or fold paper slightly in area to be cut with scissors to cut out a shape from the center of flat paper. Try to create regular patterns, e.g. scales on crocodiles, windows in sky scrapers.

- ✆ When cut as above, place contrasting color behind pierced surface.

- ✆ Curl individual lengths, alternate different colors, place multi lengths on one base strip.

- ✆ Score and twist.

Carving Extensions

Three basic types, the choice of which may depend on:

- ✆ the purpose of the carving;

- ✆ the availability of materials; and

- ✆ the age and experience of children.

Relief—where the figure stands away from the background.

In the Round—where the figure is seen from all sides.

Intaglio—where the image is cut below the background.

World Teachers Press® Resource Book

Construction - Activities

PUMPKIN CARVING

note: Suitable for older students as sharp implements are required.

- ⚅ Keeping in mind the concepts of construction/3-D/sculpture. Your challenge is to produce a _____ from a pumpkin.

❶ Lightly draw the parameters of the major features on your model.

❷ Using vegetable knives, table knives, metal spoons, chisels and craft knives, cut away and shape your carving.

❸ Exaggerate obvious features.

❹ Enhance, embellish and decorate your work.

❺ Contrast textured, patterned areas with smooth areas.

❻ Dry carefully—the overall appearance may change slightly.

❼ Spray with clear polyurethane to preserve.

❽ Use glue to add interesting features such as frayed twine, feathers, or dried leaves, if it is in keeping with the overall concept of the model.

Equipment
pumpkins, gourds, or butternuts, vegetable knives, table knives, metal spoons, chisels and craft knives

APPLE CARVING

- ⚅ This artwork will change its appearance quite dramatically from initial completion until it dries out.

❶ Select a large red or green apple and peel the skin from $\frac{1}{3}$ to $\frac{1}{2}$ of the surface.

❷ Carve a face using vegetable knife, or something similar. You will need to exaggerate the eyebrows, nose, and lips as they shrink when the apple dries.

❸ With the pieces of peel you have saved, cut shapes for the eyebrows, lips, hairline, cheekbones, etc. They will stick on the surface and adhere more firmly as the apple dehydrates.

Equipment
large apples, vegetable peeler, vegetable knife, oven, cardboard rolls

❹ Push small pieces of skin into slits to form the eyes.

❺ Leave the apples to dry or bake in an oven at a low temperature for about an hour.

❻ Complete the drying process in a warm place such as a window sill for a few days.

Display them on stands of varying heights, made from the tubes from kitchen wraps and foil.
Discuss results and see if you can create faces with specific individual personalities.

TOTEM POLES

⚅ Keeping in mind the concepts of construction/3-D/sculpture, your challenge is to produce a mask. This mask will be based on the structure of a large rectangular cardboard box (banana box size). It must be free-standing and be able to have another box mask placed on top of it. You must be able to identify your own personal/cultural reasons for the features of your creation. e.g. to scare away unwelcome night visitors, to protect newly planted seeds, to welcome the day. This may be a good discussion starter about native culture and totems.

❶ Draft out preliminary ideas on paper. Exaggerate angles, features, etc. Transfer sketch to face of box.

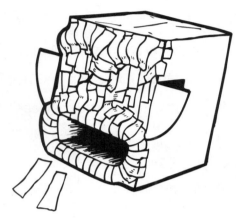

❷ Alter appearance of the box. Pierce some areas of the face and sides. Open out other areas.

❸ With sheets of scrunched up newspaper, select areas to substantialy build up facial features, e.g. lips, eyebrows, and cheekbones. Tape lightly in place.

❹ Cover the total surface area with strips of pasted newspaper. To paste newspaper:

— tear down the column, not across;

— dip the strip in wallpaper paste;

— place the strips alongside each other so each strip slightly overlays its neighbor;

— apply two layers, allowing each layer to dry, until the artwork has a firm, smooth skin all over it;

— do a final layer of pieces of white or colored paper. This final coating must be smooth, like skin.

❺ Decorate, embellish, and enhance your mask. Display as: individuals; as a totem pole type arrangement (masks can be interchanged every few days); or as a group.

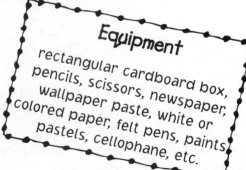
Equipment
rectangular cardboard box, pencils, scissors, newspaper, wallpaper paste, white or colored paper, felt pens, paints, pastels, cellophane, etc.

JAPANESE FISH KITE

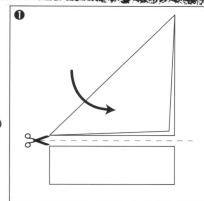

🐟 Remarkably durable—inexpensive—no skeletal frame required.

❶ Take one sheet of $8\frac{1}{2}$ x 11 photocopy paper. Carefully fold one corner over to the opposite side to square off the paper. Cut off the excess paper and keep it to one side to make the tail.

❷ Open your squared paper out and place it in front of you so the diagonal creased line is turned vertically away from you.

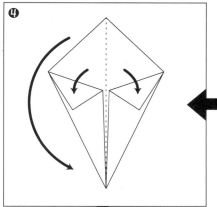

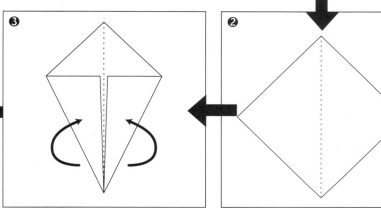

❸ Fold the lower outer edges to the center.

❹ Take each upper edge of these folds and fold it back to the outside crease.
Turn your kite so the folds are now facing away from you.

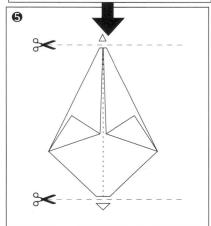

❺ Cut $\frac{1}{2}$ cm ($\frac{1}{4}$ in.) off the bottom point and cut another $\frac{1}{2}$ cm ($\frac{1}{4}$ in.) off the top point.

❻ Decorate your kite face.

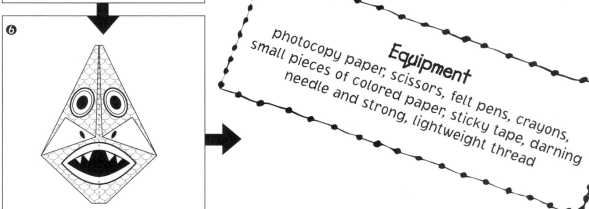

Equipment
photocopy paper, scissors, felt pens, crayons, small pieces of colored paper, sticky tape, darning needle and strong, lightweight thread

Construction – Activities

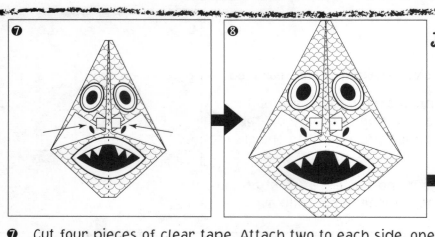

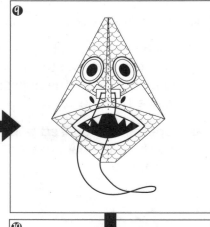

❼ Cut four pieces of clear tape. Attach two to each side, one following the line of the inner creased line and one the outer side. This will prevent tearing.

❽ Use a sharp darning needle to pierce two holes through this tape about $\frac{1}{2}$ cm ($\frac{1}{4}$ in.) in from the edge.

❾ Measure and cut a 61-cm (23 $\frac{1}{2}$ in.) length of strong, lightweight string. Using the darning needle, thread the string through the holes and tie firmly in place. Holding the string carefully in the middle, tie a small loop at the center point.

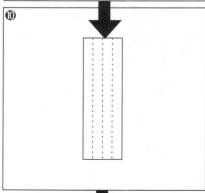

❿ Fold the strip you retained for the tail in half lengthways and then each half in half again.

⓫ Cut carefully along the creased lines so you have four strips.

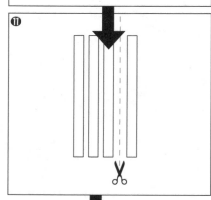

⓬ Using clear tape, join the four pieces to form one long strip—either butt the ends or overlap them.

⓭ Finally, attach the tail, using tape to the base of your kite. If your kite twirls, spins, or darts to one side, add one or two extra lengths to the tail to help stabilize it.

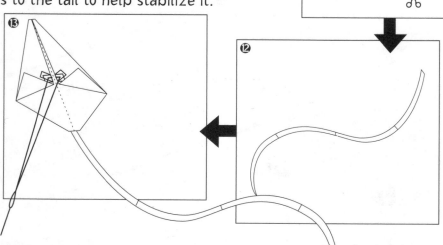

World Teachers Press® Resource Book

Construction – Activities

BIRD KITE

6 This is your chance to create your very own mobile sculpture. Be prepared to make adjustments to your creation to get it to fly. Add/shorten/lengthen tails as necessary—you don't always need a tail. Plan your design then select paper and materials for the design.

1 Select paper. It can vary in size.

2 Fold the paper width-ways, making it half its original size.

3 Your design may be based on any object that flies, e.g. birds, insects, butterflies, fish, superheroes, pigs(!) and aliens. Using your pencil, start from the top of the creased fold. Regard this area as the head of your beast! Lightly sketch out half the shape of your design. Try to avoid the shape occupying the majority of paper.

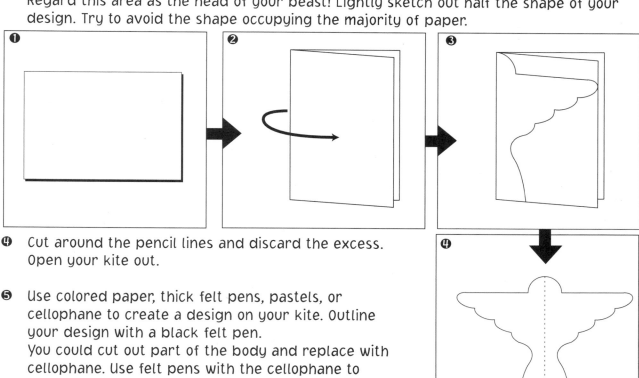

4 Cut around the pencil lines and discard the excess. Open your kite out.

5 Use colored paper, thick felt pens, pastels, or cellophane to create a design on your kite. Outline your design with a black felt pen.
You could cut out part of the body and replace with cellophane. Use felt pens with the cellophane to create designs. Your decoration should compliment the kite and not add too much weight to the overall surface area.

Equipment
manila or strong, lightweight paper, pencil, scissors, colored paper, cellophane, thick felt pens, pastels, craft sticks, masking tape, and strong, light polyester string

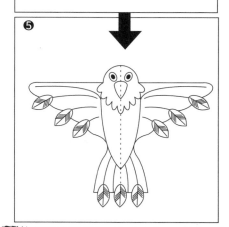

Construction – Activities

BIRD KITE cont.

❻ Turn your kite over and, depending on its size, select the size of craft sticks you will need. Construct a suitable frame for the shape of your kite. This frame should be flexible and not rigid.
The placement of the sticks (either vertically or horizontally) must span the whole length or width as a whole piece. If it doesn't, your kite will simply fold in half! Use small pieces of tape to attach the sticks.

❼ Using string, attach a bridle to your kite. There are no specific "rules" for this although 95 cm (17 $\frac{1}{2}$ in.) is a good length. It should come out from the face of the kite and enable you to tie a loop at an appropriate point so a correct flying angle can be attained.

❽ Now go and fly your kite!

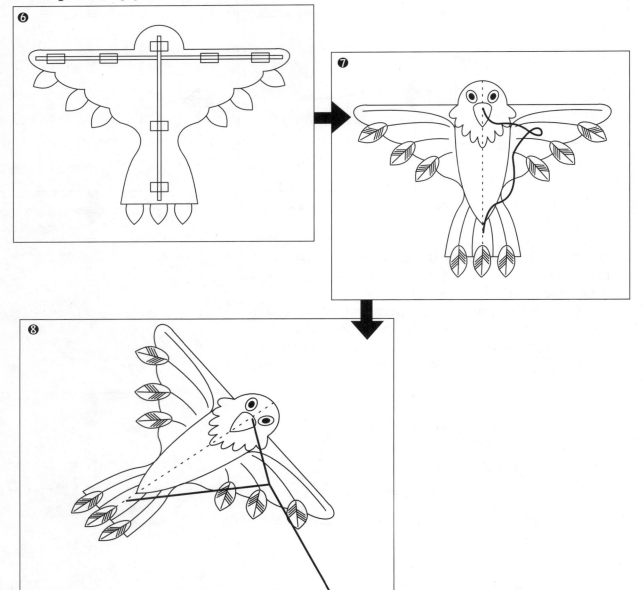

Clay – Teachers Notes

Clay allows students to express themselves through the manipulation of a 3-D medium. Encourage children to use clay as a three-dimensional process. Unlike working on a flat, 2-D surface, the shapes can be viewed from many different angles. Keep turning the sculpture around as they are working with it to make sure they are happy with the shape from whichever angle they see it.

Hints

- All clay should be plastic enough for a child to manipulate without it breaking. A simple test for plasticity is to make a sausage $1\frac{1}{2}$ cm to 2 cm diameter ($\frac{1}{2}$ in. to $\frac{3}{4}$ in.) diameter and wrap it around your finger. If it breaks, it will be difficult for the children to work with (don't worry about light cracks). This mainly occurs with found or brickyard clays, or if the clay is too dry. Overcome the problem by adding commercial clay in a controlled amount and wedging the two types together.

- If the model does not hold its shape, it is too wet.

- Sculptures built around newspaper must have a hole somewhere in the surface reaching the newspaper (to prevent explosions during firing). This prevents cracking during drying and explosions during firing. The hole can become part of the structural design.

- Wrap newspaper around cardboard cylinders when using cylinders as support. Rotate and remove cylinder within twelve hours of completing the pot to prevent cracking.

- Adding moistened sand/silt, sieved sawdust, and grog (ground-fired) clay to your clay at the mixing stage helps provide: interesting textures, strength, faster drying, and safe firing.

- All combustible materials, e.g. sawdust and newspaper, will be burnt out in the firing stage.

- Blocks of clay can be cut with nylon cord or thin wire attached to curtain rings.

- Slabs can be made by rolling clay with a rolling pin.

- While the clay is still wet, children should scratch their names, class number, and the date into the base or back of their pot or model.

- Dry clay away from direct heat sources.

- Plastic bins on castors are good for storing clay because they can be easily moved when needed.

- Laminated tabletops are not a good surface to work on because models "cling." Canvas, plastic sheets, or cutting boards are easy surfaces to work on.

- Small sponges or sandpaper are useful for finishing work when the model/pot is dry.

- Glazes will not adhere to work that has been touched with greasy fingers or allowed to gather dust.

Clay – Preparation

EQUIPMENT

Roadside cuttings, earth works, riverbeds, basement excavations and edges of stores of water are good sources for found clay.

Dry Found Clay

- Pound with a wooden mallet until broken down as fine as possible.
- Throw clay through a screen to remove stones, sticks, and other matter.
- Arrange sieved clay in a mound with a well in the middle and pour water into the cavity a little at a time.

Mixing Process: Pull dry clay from the mound into the water. Work more dry clay into the water until the moisture is absorbed. Gradually mix all the clay to the proper consistency.

Moist Found Clay

- Soak in water for a few days and drain off excess.
- To get the clay into working condition "wedge" it (i.e. cut the clay in two with nylon or thin wire and work the pieces together again to form one piece using the same movements with which you would knead bread) on plasterboard or warm concrete in the sun. Adding sand or sieved sawdust at this stage may speed the process.

Mixing Clay: Clays from varying sources can be mixed together by vigorous wedging. The new clay must have no evidence of streaks from the two original clays. Inadequate mixing may result in models shattering in the kiln. Mixing of clays can extend the amount of clay available as well as improve the plasticity of found clays.

Commercial Clay: Shop around, some sources are much cheaper than others. Commercial clays don't generally need any formal preparation, though you may wish to "wedge" the clay. Knead the clay as if it was dough for bread: this removes any air bubbles. Moisten fingers on a damp sponge if the clay starts to dry.

Other Materials

- Plastic tablecloths can be shaken outside at the end of the lesson. Plenty of newspaper is an adequate alternative.
- Pieces of cardboard about 45 cm x 45 (12 $\frac{1}{2}$ in. x 12 $\frac{1}{2}$ in.) help define territory, facilitate the lifting of damp models, and discourages the use of excess water.
- Sponges stay damp in plastic containers. Teacher only adds more water to sponges.
- Large bucket with warm water for washing hands prevents blocked drains. Tip the dirty water on the garden.
- Tools—knives, craft sticks, wire, nails, forks, string, stones, meat tenderizers, rolling pins, bottles, matches, buttons, toothpicks and wooden blocks.
- Large, strong plastic bags to store the clay tied securely to keep the clay damp. Smaller plastic bags, e.g. supermarket bags, for storing unfinished work.

Extension and Research

Collect a range of photographs and/or actual objects which have been made from clay (i.e. sculptures, pots, beads, vessels, etc.). Children can help form the collection. Make sure there are items from: other countries, cultures and time periods. Look at each item individually and classify them according to whether they are mainly "functional" or "decorative." Which items are both?

Look at certain items and discuss them in terms of: decoration (e.g. glazing, burnishing, painting, or relief work), "form", texture and make comparisons between objects from different countries.

Clay – Skills

Clay Slip

⊚ Slip is powdered clay mixed with water to a consistency of thick cream. It is applied, like glue, to two edges of clay that are joined. Score edges with a sharp object and use a brush to apply the slip.

Joining

⊚ Slip method: When joining two pieces of clay, moisten the surface, scratch it, or score it and work the two pieces together firmly. There should be no evidence of where the two pieces originally met.

⊚ Scoring: Score both surfaces of the clay and press together.

⊚ As our skin covers our appendages so should the surface of the model give a smooth appearance.

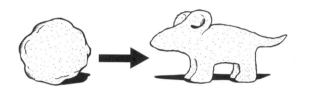

Squeezing

⊚ Squeeze the model from one lump of clay so there are no joins.

Applied Pieces

⊚ Use a plastic squeeze bottle with a pointed nozzle to apply dots, or a trail of clay slip.

⊚ Push small pieces of clay through a sieve or garlic press and apply the long strands to your model with clay slip.

⊚ Cut out shapes and apply to the model with clay slip.

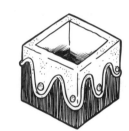

Imprinting

⊚ Use found objects to apply a variety of textures by pressing, rolling, and scratching.

Decorating Tools

⊚ Found objects such as:
   textured material
   buttons
   skewers
   popsicle sticks
   pencils
   textured cylinders
   felt-tip pens

Clay – Activities

COIL POTS

Demonstrate how to construct a coil pot. Suggest either a fat, tubby shape for a pot-plant or a tall tumbler for a pencil jar. Finished project walls should be no more than 2 cm ($^3/_4$ in.) or it will blow up when fired.

❶ Form a ball and flatten it for the base.

❷ Roll small sausages fairly thinly to make coils. Attach each to the previous round by pinching together on the inside and then smoothing it out. Leave the outside natural looking in its coils, but make sure the coils are firmly joined on the inside.

❸ When the pot has reached the desired height, the coils can be decorated by pushing buttons, etc. into the clay.

❹ If the pot is not completed in one session, wrap it in a plastic bag. The coil pot will take about two weeks to dry before firing.

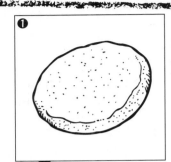
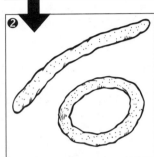
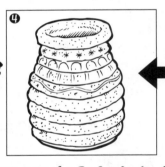

Equipment
clay, water, brush, scratching tool (e.g. toothpick), decorating tools, plastic bag

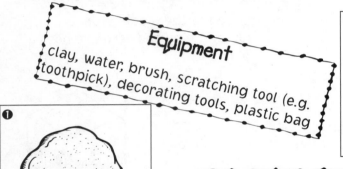

ANIMALS

❶ Begin with one lump of clay about 6 cm (2 $^1/_2$ in.) in diameter.

❷ By squeezing and molding, make the legs, head, ears and tail of your chosen animal.

❸ Facial details and texture for fur or scales can be scratched in with a toothpick. Balance the animal so it can stand on its own. (There should be no adding or joining of clay in this process.)

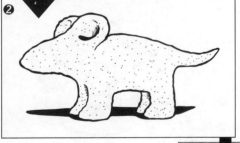

Equipment
clay, toothpicks

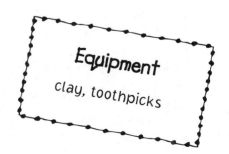

Clay – Activities

MASK

❶ Take a piece of clay about the size of a tennis ball and roll it flat to a thickness of 1 cm ($^1/_4$–$^1/_2$ in.)

❷ Either leave the edges ragged as it has been rolled, or cut it into the shape you want.

❸ Cut out interesting shaped holes for the eyes and mouth. Add clay (using slip method) to form a nose, eyebrows, chin, and decorations.

❹ Use tools to make textures and patterns.

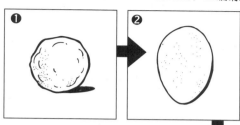

Equipment

clay, water, brush, decorating tools, rolling pin, butter knife

SLAB WORK–Tiles

❶ Take a piece of clay about the size of a tennis ball and roll it flat to a thickness of 1 cm ($^1/_4$–$^1/_2$ in.)

❷ Cut into a tile shape.

❸ Decide how you will decorate the tile. Add layers of clay using slip. Use tools to add texture and patterns to the tile.

Equipment

clay, water, brush, decorating tools, butter knife, rolling pin

Pots

❶ Take a piece of clay about the size of a tennis ball and roll it to about 1 cm ($^1/_4$–$^1/_2$ in.) thickness (no less).

❷ Cut out five even squares and attach them together using the slip method. (The squares may be textured for ease in joining.)

❸ The edges of the pot may be rounded and the outside of the pot may be decorated with relief and textural work.

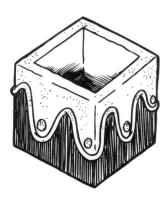

Clay – Activities

PINCH POTS

❶ Pinch pots are made from a small (golf ball size) ball of clay, pinched with your thumb inside and two fingers pressing against the outside, moving around as you pinch.

Equipment
clay, brush, sieve, garlic crusher, water

❷ Two pinch pots joined together using the slip method can form the basis for a hollow head shapes.

❸ The join needs to be well attached and a mouth cut out.

❹ Features can be added and hair can be made with strands of clay put through a sieve or a garlic crusher.

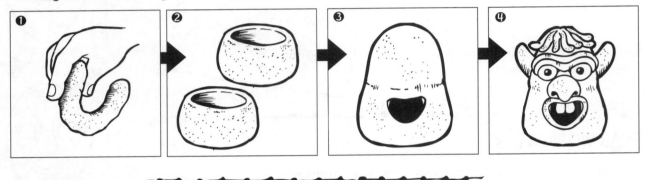

JEWELRY

❶ Pendants, beads and buttons can be made into practically any shape, small and large. Use a nail or piece of dowel to make the holes in the appropriate places.

❷ The jewelry should be interesting and original with good use of shapes and textures and, later, color from either paint or glazes.

❸ Leather thonging or string can be used to hang pendants and beads.

Equipment
clay, skewers, decorating tools, paints, glazes, leather thonging, string

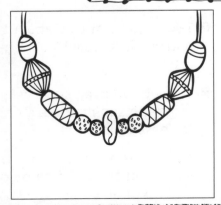

Clay – Activities

MAKE A MEAL

❶ Model clay to make a realistic looking plate of food (e.g. sausages, potato and broccoli). Let the children decide what their meal should consist of.

❷ Use acrylic paint to finish the work.

❸ The work can be displayed on a table as a large banquet.

Equipment

clay, decorating tools, acrylic paint

DRAGON

❶ Crumple newspaper into a ball and tape around it. Roll marble size balls of clay and flatten them over the ball of newspaper, overlapping and smoothing as you go.

❷ Roll a sausage about 20 cm (8 in.) long and 2 cm ($^3/_4$ in.) thick. Cut it into four equal pieces to make the legs and feet. Bend each into a foot and cut in the toes. Be creative; bend the toes, add claws, etc. Attach the feet to the body by scoring the edges, pressing together and smoothing the joins. (Do not add water!) Use slip after scoring

❸ Make another sausage for the neck. Model the details of the head before scoring and attaching the neck to the body. Cut it on the angle you want it to be attached.

❹ To make the row of plates down its back and its tail, roll a long sausage and pinch it with your fingers. Attach the row by pressing and scoring.

❺ Encourage experimentation with texture; skewers, pencils, felt-tip pens and knife points. Try tiny balls of clay rolled and flattened on the dinosaur with a pencil tip, or scales made separately and overlapped.

note: Poke a hole into the body between the feet or else it will explode when fired. Let it dry naturally for about two weeks before firing.

Equipment

clay, newspaper, decorating tools

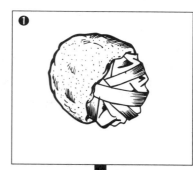

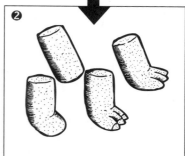

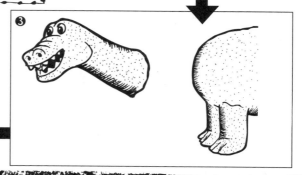

Clay – Activities

UGLY MUG

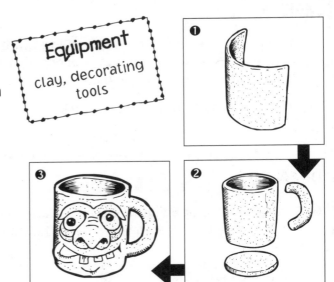

Equipment

clay, decorating tools

6 Look at gargoyles, trolls and gnomes. Discuss exaggerated facial features.

1 Roll clay to 2 cm (³/₄ in.) thickness and cut a rectangle about 10 cm x 15 cm (4 in. x 6 in.) Join to make a cylinder.

2 Make a round base and attach it to the cylinder (using scoring plus slip). Press a thin coil into the inside to help the join. Make a handle if you like or incorporate your ugly figure into the handle.

3 Make grotesque facial features to attach to the mug.

PERSON IN AN OVERCOAT

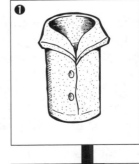

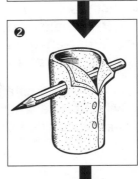

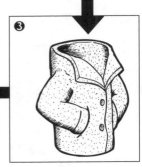

1 Roll clay to 1 cm (¹/₂ in.) thickness. Cut out a rectangle approximately 10 cm x 15 cm (4 in. x 6 in.). Roll this around so the ends meet and join it to form a coat, leaving a few centimeters (inches) at the top to make a collar.
A base can be added to it by sitting it on a rolled slab, cutting the shape out then sticking it to the lower edge of the coat.

2 Make sleeves by rolling the clay flat and then forming it into tubes. Press holes into the coat with a pencil.

3 Squeeze the sleeves onto the coat, making sure the joins are smooth.

4 Make a head with a neck to act as a cork so it can be removed from the coat and act as a storage pot. (The head should be hollowed out.) Discuss the position of the features and how to build out a nose and chin. Use various tools to help create a unique and interesting character.

Equipment

clay, pencil, decorating tools

Painting – Teachers Notes

Painting may be seen to many as too messy for the classroom, but with a little organization and pre-planning, it can be an enjoyable experience for both teacher and students. If you really can't bear the mess inside, choose your days and paint outside!

Painting, with its large arm movements and emphasis on leaving big brush strokes, allows children a freedom not apparent in many other areas of either classroom work or art activity.

Encourage children to experiment with color mixing, choosing and using tools to apply paint with, and finding ways of creating textural effects. This will be far more exciting and beneficial than for the teacher to tell them exactly what to paint.

Hints

For younger students, paints in bottles with several brushes for each color. For older students, a palette per group with red, blue, yellow, white, black and several palettes for mixing.

- Teach skills and encourage discovery through experimentation.
- Continue questioning and skills teaching with individuals as they work.
- Encourage completion—even if it takes several lessons. Remember there is no such thing as a permanent mistake in painting. Changes can be made when the paint is dry.
- Mount, discuss and display.

Mixing Colors

- Mix black with primary colors to make different shades and white to make different tints.
- Mix primary colors to get secondary colors. For example,
  Red and yellow make orange,
  Blue and yellow make green,
  Red and blue make purple...

Equipment

newspaper for desks, old shirts, paper of various thickness, various brushes, manila or copy paper, mixing palettes, water containers, acrylic and tempera paints, string, wool, chalk

Extension and Research

Try to relate painting techniques which the children are being led to discover, to other artwork.

For example, if you are emphasizing texture, look at Van Gogh's "Sunflowers" and lead the children to discover that he laid paint on very thickly, left it without blending it and used several different yellows in one flower.

Have examples of paintings by local, national and international artists. Color prints are good (the larger the better). Black and white prints are of no use for color mixing exercises.

Have samples of contemporary art for children to appreciate. Keep an eye out in magazines for any paintings on topics your class might study and surround with artwork. Your local library may have framed prints to loan.

Painting – Skills

Techniques for Students

❻ Children should experiment with textures that can be made and repeated to form patterns.

❻ Children should achieve wet to dry brush effects.

❻ Children should understand the effects of different sized brushes.

❻ Children should know the types of textures which can be formed by:

Stippling

❻ Multiple dry brush applications

Dry Brush Technique

❻ Use no water and very little paint to produce scratchy lines

Blobbing

❻ Create multiple wet brush applications using a soft bristled brush

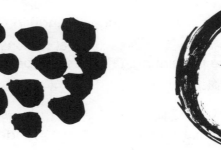

Long Dry Strokes

Rotating Strokes

❻ Brush using circular motions

Rolling

❻ Turn a wet brush in rolling motions.

Long Wet Strokes

World Teachers Press® Resource Book

Painting – Activities

FINGER PAINTING and MONOPRINTING

EQUIPMENT

smooth, protected surface to work on, wallpaper paste, tempera powder or finger paint, newsprint for taking monoprint, music with a variety of rhythmic patterns, sponges or damp cloths

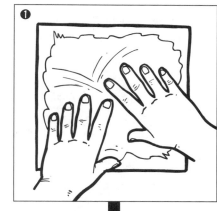

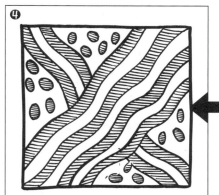
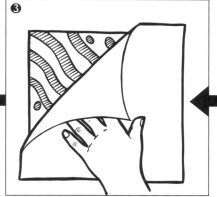
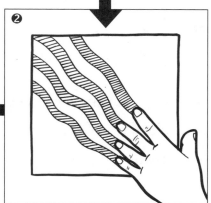

❶ Begin with only a small amount of two colors. Spread paste and paint over painting surface.

❷ Use both hands. Experiment with palms, finger tips and knuckles. Make sweeping, jagged, smooth, scaly, or ruffled patterns.

❸ and ❹ Take a monoprint of your image by placing a piece of newsprint on wet picture, pressing and removing immediately.

Extensions

❻ Make pictures using lots of colors.

❼ Use finger painting to make backgrounds for large group pictures—it is ideal for representing sky, grass and foliage. Three-dimensional objects can be stuck on while it is still wet.

Painting – Activities

DRY BRUSH ANIMALS

This dry brush technique is very useful in painting some animals. As with all creative endeavors, children must have experiences to paint about, so make a study of a furry or hairy animal, perhaps in conjunction with a "pet day" or an excursion to the zoo.

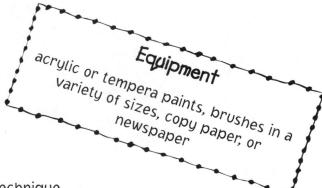

Equipment
acrylic or tempera paints, brushes in a variety of sizes, copy paper, or newspaper

❶ Discuss and experiment with dry brush technique.

❷ Look at an animal and closely observe the texture, patterns, direction of fur and shape of the head.

❸ Sketch an outline of the basic shape in chalk.

❹ Use dry brush technique mixing several colors to show variations in the animals' fur.

❺ Use a detail brush to add teeth, eyes, etc.

RANDOM SHAPES, COLORS AND EFFECTS

❶ Discuss methods of applying paint, blending colors and different shapes.

❷ Make at least four random folds in your paper to make an interesting 3-D effect.

❸ Leave the paper folded and paint on top of and under folds using the techniques discussed.

❹ When dry, stitch some folds together.

Equipment
poster board or manila paper, acrylic paints, a variety of brushes, newspaper, string, wool, metallic thread and needles, other paint application tools

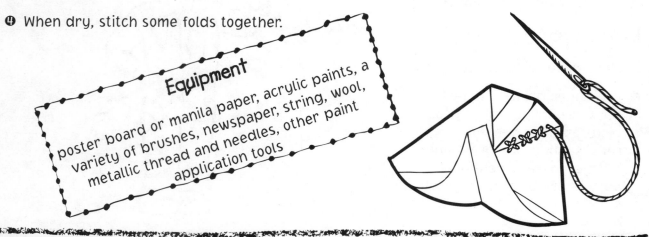

Painting – Activities

KORU SHAPES

The Maori people of New Zealand use a scroll shape, which leads to a hoop design, frequently in their carving and tattooing. The scroll shape is linked to the New Zealand fern reaching for the light, striving for perfection and symbolic of new life. The koru shape represents strength, growth and new life for the Maori people.

⚅ Demonstrate making the koru shape.

⚁ It must start from the paper's edge or from another koru. It may be a different size or be wider at the base but it does not change shape.

⚅ The knob on the end is round, it is not shaped like a field hockey stick.

Equipment

acrylic or tempera paints, newsprint, a variety of brushes, chalk, newspaper, cartridge, crayon, felt pens

❶

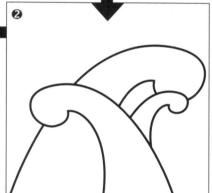
❹

❸

❷

❶ Design, in chalk, koru shapes for every family member. Think about sizes in relation to people.

❷ Some koru shapes should start from another koru, forming new negative shapes. Some can start from two sides of the paper.

❸ Choose and mix colors which relate to your family members and paint shapes accordingly.

❹ When dry, add patterns in paint/crayon/felt pens to enhance the koru shapes and/or some negative spaces.

Negative Image

Image from Two Sides

Painting – Activities

PORTRAIT PAINTING

❶ Lightly chalk in head and features.

❷ Look carefully at where your different features are in relation to each other. Our eyes are almost exactly half way down our head and our ears are positioned just below the eye line.

❸ The background should show tones from dark to light and light to dark. Experiment with color mixing and consider that the color of your hair needs to contrast with the background. Paint the background first, this will ensure that it looks like it's actually behind the person, not creeping around over the top.

❹ Mix and experiment with paint for your skin colors. Emphasize shaded areas and highlights to show the contour of a surface.

❺ Use several colors when painting your hair. Look at how your hair grows. Short spiky hair—short spiky strokes, long flowing hair—long flowing strokes.

Emphasize using the most suitable-sized brush for the job.

Equipment

chalk, acrylic paint, newspaper, variety of brush sizes, half sheet of poster board or full sheet of copy paper

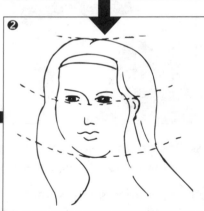

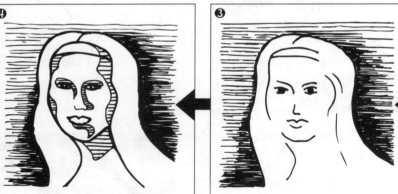

World Teachers Press® Resource Book

Painting – Activities

LANDSCAPE PAINTING

Look initially at your immediate landscape. Observe colors, textures and landforms. Discuss how to create the textures we see. Experiment with ways of painting grass, rocks, smooth hills, craggy mountains, water in creeks, streams, rivers and lakes, or whatever geographical features are in your landscape. Look at a variety of landscape paintings and discuss the techniques used to show mood, color, and texture.

Equipment
cardboard frames, acrylic paint, variety of brushes, other tools, half sheet of poster board or a full sheet of copy paper, and a fine day to paint outside!

❶ Talk about the environment you are going to paint (land, water, sky). Find words to describe the mood it brings to you.

❷ Now choose one cool color and one warm color which compliment the mood you want to portray in your painting.

Hint: Cool colors come from the blue end of the spectrum i.e. blues, greens, greys and warm colors come from the red end of the spectrum i.e. red, oranges, yellows, browns, pinks. Remember that if you choose green as your cool color, for instance, there are infinite different green hues to be mixed.

❸ Think about textures, shapes and patterns that will best describe the mood, e.g. exaggerate some shapes and textures, simplify shapes. Decide what tools and techniques will be most effective.

❹ Use a light cardboard frame (about half or a quarter of the size of the paper you are painting on), to help select your composition. Hold it out in front of you and look at it in a similar way you look through a camera lens deciding what is going to be in your picture and what is going to be left out. Move it around until you find a composition you like; this is what you will transfer onto paper.

❺ As you paint, always keep in mind the "mood" or "feeling" you want people to experience when they look at your painting.

Fabric and Fiber - Teachers Notes

Creating in fabric and fiber can provide children with a tactile experience in the art program. Choosing and deciding on fabrics, textures and colors to use along with threads and yarns, provides opportunities for discussion and problem-solving by the student. Painting and dyeing fabric creates another opportunity for using skills learned in painting and dyeing on paper.

Hints

- Demonstrate threading and stitching. Children can plan a picture of themselves to be made of fabric on burlap. They can cut out their clothes from material and stitch them on. They can cut out faces, arms, and legs from plain materials or paper and glue them on. They can sew buttons for eyes and glue wool for hair. If you combine gluing and stitching it does not become a chore which takes the children hours of work. These can be made into wall hangings by stapling or gluing cotton strips to the top and bottom and attaching a yarn handle.

- Each child can sew a button onto a small square of material and these can then be glued to a large shape, e.g. a fish with each square forming a scale.

- Children can print on material with screen printing inks or just acrylic paint and, when dry, stitch around parts to make them stand out or they can stitch on crayoned lines and paint the shapes later. Batting can be pinned under the material and stitched around the shapes required.

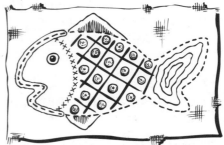

- Simple shapes can be cut out and stitched together to become toys or pincushions.

- Make group pictures on large pieces of burlap working together on the stitching and gluing.

- Draw outlines of animals or other shapes in crayon and stitch thick wool around the lines.

Extension and Research

Encourage children to seek and find, in their families and communities, craftspeople and artists who work in fabric and fiber.

Check:
- Local spinners and weavers' guilds
- Embroiderers' guild
- Soft toy makers
- Soft sculpture makers
- Clothes designers
- Fabric printers
- Screen printers
- Museum collections of old embroidery, lace, samplers and clothing
- Indonesian batik fabric
- Collect printed fabrics and clothes showing various arrangements and motifs
- Encourage children to be aware of patterns in fabric and how they are printed

Fabric and Fiber – Skills

Stitching

Blanket Stitch

Chain Stitch

Cross Stitch

Detatched Chain Stitch

Feather Stitch

Fly Stitch

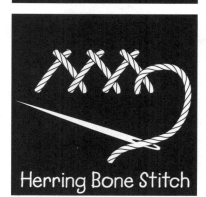

Herring Bone Stitch

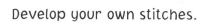

Stem Stitch

Running Stitch

Sheaf Stitch

Develop your own stitches.

Fabric and Fiber – Activities

SOFT SCULPTURE FACES

⟲ Show the class an example of a soft sculpture face.

ℯ Demonstrate how to draw the face—sparse detail only required. Revise the proportions of the face. Students draw a large face on their paper. No neck is required. Go over the pencil lines with black felt pen when drawn.

❶ Wet a piece of cheesecloth and lay it over the drawing. Black felt will show through. Paint the face using heat-set dyes. Allow to dry.

❷ Cut each child a piece of batting to fit their face.

❸ Sew around the edge of the face. If possible use parent help with a sewing machine to machine stitch around each one.

❹ Demonstrate how to sew around the eyes—either right around or slightly above to form eyelids down one side of the nose, around and into the nostrils, across the center of the lips if they are closed (or across the bottom of the top lip and the top of the bottom lip if open).

❺ Trim the cheesecloth to about 3 cm (1 ¼ in.) from the stitches and trim the batting very close to the stitching.

❻ Children then pin the excess material to the back and stitch it to the batting. Use all the faces together for a display. For example: they can be looking out windows or in a bus, plane, train, etc. which can be made from burlap or cardboard. They can be stitched or glued.

Equipment

newspaper, black felt pens, brushes, cheesecloth, water containers, batting 20 cm x 25 cm (8in. x 10 in.), heat-set dyes— white, yellow, red, brown, black, ochre, green

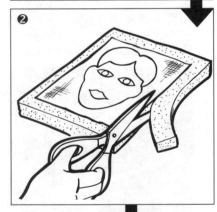

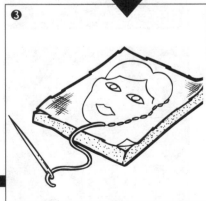

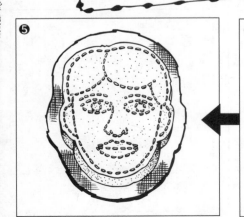

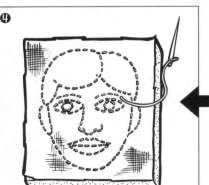

World Teachers Press® Resource Book

Fabric and Fiber – Activities

SOFT SCULPTURE CREATURES

❶ Roll the batting into tight rolls and stitch. Wire may be included for strength.

❷ Stitch batting together to make the framework.

❸ Place the framework on two sheets of muslin and cut around the shape, leaving 2 cm ($^3/_4$ in.) to spare.

❹ Stretch the muslin over the frame and stitch.

❺ Sew features onto the model, decorate.

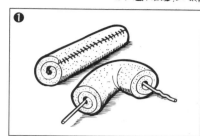

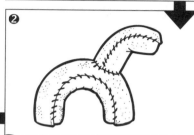

Equipment

batting cut-offs, thread, sequins and buttons, muslin, lacing wire, gold and silver thread, needles, school dyes

TIE-DYEING

◉ Show samples of different techniques and discuss how to achieve them. Prepare the cloth as follows.

❶ Follow instructions on dye packet and soak tied cloth for one hour. If you wish to add a second color, leave ties on and add more before soaking in a second darker color. Use dye fastener to speed up process if desired.

❷ Rinse out excess dye until water runs clear. Untie your fabric and wash in warm, soapy water. Rinse well, dry, then iron.

Fabric Use

◔ Use the design as a basis for adding stitching.

◉ Use to cut up for fabric collage.

◔ Stencil on top to accentuate the patterns.

◉ Make into clothes, e.g. vest, hat, shorts.

Equipment

cotton fabric (washed), pebbles or buttons, cold water dyes, string or rubber bands, one bucket and a pair of gloves for each color

Circles
Hold center of fabric and smooth to the outside. Tie tightly in several places.

Random Design
Scrunch fabric into a ball and tie tightly all around.

Stripes
Pleat fabric into a fan. Tie tightly in several, evenly spaced places.

Small Circles
Tie pebbles or buttons in several places.

Fabric and Fiber – Activities

BATIK

⚬ Batik is the method of using hot wax on fabric to resist dye. Use of hot wax and dyes may require small groups and/or additional adult supervision.

Organization

⚬ The wax in the pan must be just at the smoking stage to be hot enough. Do not let it overheat. Stress the importance of being careful. Hot wax burns!

⚬ Have one group set up with the pan in the center with room for six to eight children.

⚬ Have a second group set up with several layers of newspaper and dyes in the center. Children move to the dyeing table from the waxing area, hang their fabric to dry then go off to design their larger piece of work.

⚬ It will only take a short time for each child to get a practice piece of about 12 cm (4 in.) completed (1 or $1\frac{1}{2}$ sessions for the class). If there is a hold up, children can start designing their larger piece. The whole project will probably take about four sessions.

⚬ When fabric is completely dry, wax needs to be removed. Older children can organize themselves to do this. With younger children it may be less messy for teachers or parents to do it for them.

⚬ Fabric is put into a bucket with about half a cup of washing powder on top. Boiling water is poured in and fabric swished around with a stick. Fabric needs to be fished out from the edge of the bucket and rinsed thoroughly twice in cold water. Water from the bucket must **not** be poured down the drain, (the wax will harden and block it).

Flour and Water Paste Batik

For younger children the same process can be used using flour and water paste in squeeze bottles. When the fabric is dry it prevents the paint (not dye) from seeping through and can be crumpled and picked off to leave white fabric lines.

Cold Wax Batik

Dipping is not suitable for cold wax as soaking in water removes cold wax. Painting the dyes on is most suitable when using cold wax.

Fabric and Fiber – Activities

BATIK cont.

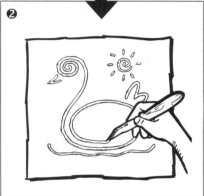

Equipment

paraffin wax (add 25% beeswax to make less brittle when dry), old brushes. commercial cold water dyes (use instructions from packet), electric frying pan, cotton fabric, lots of newspaper

❶ Draw outlines of your design on newsprint and trace over them with a permanent marker. (This can be placed under the fabric and will show through to be used as a guide.)

❷ Demonstrate application of wax with brushes. Children can practice on a scrap of fabric.

❸ Wax your design onto fabric. Brush on dyes to color the design. Consider your colors and experiment with mixing and allowing some to bleed together.

❹ When fabric is dry, wax needs to be removed per previous instructions on page 32.

Using more than one color to dip

⑥ Use cold water dyes and follow instructions on the packet or as per recipe. Choose three colors, for example, yellow, green and blue.

❶ First, wax the areas of your design you wish to stay white.

❷ Soak the fabric in the lightest color, (i.e. yellow) for 60 minutes.

❸ Take out and rinse until the water runs clear. Leave to dry.

❹ Wax over the areas you wish to stay yellow.

❺ Soak in the second color (i.e. green) for 60 minutes.

❻ Remove, rinse, and leave to dry once again.

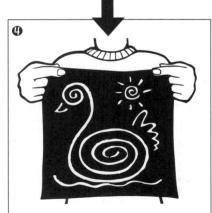

❼ Wax over the areas you wish to stay green. Soak in the darkest color (i.e. blue) for 60 minutes.

❽ Remove, rinse, and remove the wax.

Print Making – Teachers Notes

Print making requires some effort on the teacher's part to establish sound routines in the organization of equipment and setting up of the room. However, the rewards are immense when you see the faces of the children light up in wonder as they peel off their first print.

Hints

⚅ Cover all tables with newspaper and all children with art shirts.

⚇ Have one cardboard or linoleum inking plate, one roller and one tube of water-based printing ink per group set up at the end of the table.

⚇ At the other end of the table have a clean roller and a pile of newsprint or copy paper.

⚅ Stress that only the teacher touches the tubes of ink. Squeeze about 2 cm ($^3/_4$ in.) onto the plate. Demonstrate how to evenly cover the roller and stress that every part of the plate must be inked up evenly.

⚇ Establish the procedure of inking their plates then carrying them carefully to the clean end of the group. Demonstrate how the clean edges will get inky if a print is taken at the inky area.

⚅ To take a good print, place paper carefully on top of the plate and roll evenly and firmly to the edges with the clean roller.

⚇ When printed, children write their name on the edge and remove the print to the drying area.

⚅ Hang a length of string, above children's head height, from one wall to another to make a clothesline to dry prints on.

⚇ Children can then move to another color and take other prints. When they are making prints of more than one color, it is important the first print be dry before the next is added.

⚅ The spike on the roller is for standing it up when not in use. When in use, emphasize that the spike should point up to the sky or it may rip the paper.

⚇ Children's work should always be named, preferably signed themselves, but not with a thick obtrusive marker that interferes with the composition of the artwork. The standard way for print makers to sign their work is done in pencil below the work like so:

3/6	Night Flight	Kay Stent	June 97
number in edition	print title	artist's signature	date

⚅ Prints are not trimmed right to the edge. Work to be exhibited on the wall should be mounted approximately and displayed in such a way and in such a place which acknowledges respect for the work.

Equipment

newspapers, water-based printing inks (one color per group), sheets of heavy cardboard or linoleum about 20 cm x 40 cm (8 in. x 15 in.) (use as inking plates, one per color required), piles of $^1/_4$ sheets of newsprint or half sheets of copy paper.

Print Making – Activities

STRING PRINTS

❶ Use a crayon to sketch out the planned picture on heavy cardboard.

❷ Trace over the outline with white glue.

❸ Allow time for it to get tacky (about two minutes) then press wool or twine into the glue. Place thread close together for solid effects and further apart for linear patterns. Allow a day for the glue to dry thoroughly.

❹ Make a print. (See page 34, teachers notes.)

(See page 34, teachers notes.)

Equipment

thick cardboard for plate, crayon or pencil, standard printing equipment, white glue, newspaper, wool, or twine

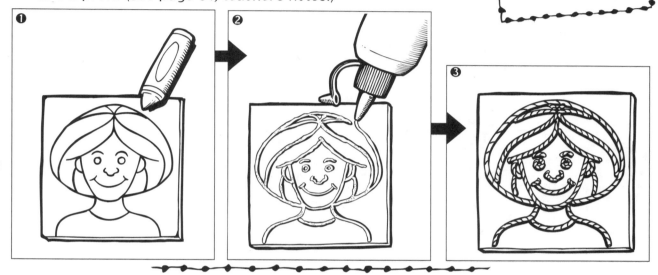

TEXTURE PRINTS

❶ Cut your textured materials into the desired shapes and lay them onto the cardboard plate.

❷ Make additions and changes until you are happy with the arrangement. Do not add more than two layers.

❸ Glue the materials down and wait for the glue to dry.

❹ Make a print. (See page 34, teachers notes.)

(See page 34, teachers notes.)

Equipment

thick cardboard for plate, white glue, scissors, standard printing equipment, a variety of textured materials, e.g. lace, net, corduroy fabric, burlap, textured wallpaper, string, wool, corrugated cardboard, leaves

Print Making – Activities

STENCILS

❻ A stencil is a hole cut in paper that allows ink or paint to pass through. Its main **advantage** is its ability to duplicate.

❶ Take a piece of paper, fold it and cut out a shape.
Keep both pieces.

❷ Place the positive shape, (the cut out piece) on your paper.

❸ Use the stencil brush in a vertical position only. Dab (don't brush) around the edge of the cut out shapes. To change color, change brushes (do not wash until the end of the lesson).

❹ Try repeating the shape in several places on your paper. Don't add any more ink and each shape will become lighter.
The same process can be used with the negative shape (the background piece).

Equipment

photocopy or computer paper for cutting stencils, scissors or knives, stencil brush (old paintbrushes with the bristles cut down), printing inks rolled onto a square of lino or cardboard, copy paper or newsprint to work on

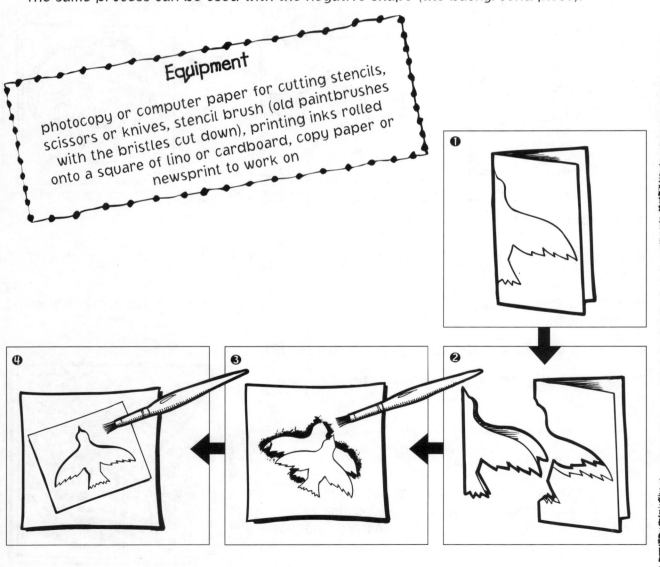

Print Making – Activities

CARDBOARD PRINTS

❶ Make a drawing of your subject on thin cardboard. It should take up about $^2/_3$ of the cardboard.

❷ Cut it out and divide it, placing each segment onto heavy cardboard with a small gap between each.

❸ Glue down with white glue.

❹ Use the left over scraps of thin card to add details and decorations.

❺ Make a print. (See page 34, teachers notes.)

Equipment

standard printing equipment, white glue, pencils, thick cardboard (about 15 x 30 cm (6 in. x 12 in.)), thin cardboard (about 15 x 30 cm (6 in. x 12 in.)), scissors

 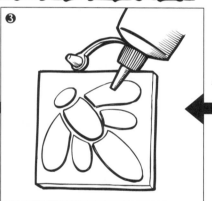 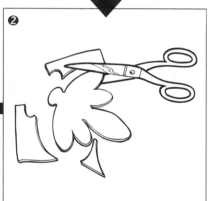

CRAYON RUBBINGS

❶ Prepare a printing plate by gluing flat metal or manufactured objects onto a piece of copy paper.

❷ The textured block is placed face down in the center of $^1/_4$ or $^1/_2$ sheet of newsprint. Paper is folded over the block and creased firmly over the edges to hold it in place.

❸ Rub the side of the crayons on newsprint to remove any dirt.

❹ Firmly rub the lightest color over the whole plate with the crayon on its side. Use firm pushing and pulling strokes. Repeat this action with the other colors on top. Try taking several rubbings using different color combinations.

Equipment

thick cardboard, white glue, flat manufactured objects (e.g. cardboard shapes, wire), three crayons, newsprint, flat natural objects (e.g. leaves, feathers, sand)

Print Making – Activities

STAMP PRINTING

❶ Use a paintbrush to paint the end of the object, or put paint on sponges for stamping the objects into.

❷ Stamp several times from each dipping onto the paper.

❸ Use the skill acquired to make pictures or to create patterns and designs: border patterns, circular patterns (start from the center), random patterns.

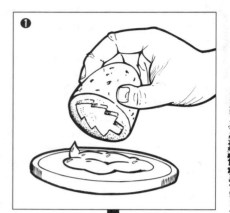

Equipment

vegetables, cardboard shapes, sponges, cardboard edges, acrylic paint, brushes,
newspaper, newsprint or copy paper, found objects (e.g. bottle tops, bark, shells, building blocks)

INDENTED PRINTING

❶ Make a light preliminary sketch, with pencil, onto cardboard.

❷ Once you are satisfied with the image, go over it with a ball point pen pressing very firmly to make a dent in the cardboard.

Make a print. (See page 34, teachers notes.)

❻ This is a linear process so the use of various types of lines is important. (You may want to practice making different sorts of lines before you begin.) Lines can be used to create different textures which imply different surfaces e.g. hair, scales, veins, and cracks.

Equipment

ball point pens and pencils, cardboard (not too flimsy and preferably shiny), standard printing equipment

Print Making - Activities

SCREEN PRINTING

๑ Screen printing follows on logically from stencilling but is messier and takes more time to clean up.

Organization

๑ Keep the room well-ventilated or, if possible, work outside on tables.

๑ One screen print area for each color. Set up a newspaper pad of about six newspapers and cover the rest of the tables as well. Have a plastic lid handy for placing a wet squeegee on.

๑ A screen, textile ink, squeegee, spoon, plastic lid for each color table.

๑ Get children to work in pairs; one to help by holding the screen.

๑ Have a clothesline to hang completed prints on.

๑ Screens have to be thoroughly cleaned. You may need to use soap and a dishwashing brush or sponge as well.

๑ Don't leave screens to clean them later. They won't come clean and will need to be replaced.

๑ If children get textile ink on their clothes, it will come off if still wet and plenty of water is applied.

❶ Cut out stencil carefully. Do not cut background paper. Place fabric on pad of unfolded newspapers.

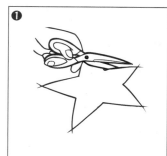

❷ Place stencil on top of fabric and the screen on top of stencil.

❸ Spoon textile ink across the top edge of the screen. Carefully and evenly drag it down the screen with the squeegee. This is best done in pairs.

❹ Remove the squeegee and carefully lift the screen off.

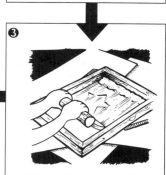

Equipment

art shirts for all, four silk screens for a class, four squeegees to drag the ink across the screen, heat-set textile inks and spoons, lots of newspaper, craft knives and scissors, fabric, cutting boards, paper for cutting stencils from (manila/computer paper), must be at least as big as the screen

Print Making - Activities

SCREEN PRINTING cont.

What can you do with screen prints?

Screen 1   Screen 2

- Place the screen down again in several places and make a repeated pattern.
- When it is dry you could paint colors or patterns on the unprinted parts of your design.
- Print it on a T-shirt.
- Put batting underneath it and machine or hand-stitch around the lines.
- Make a group picture with everyone printing onto one large sheet.
- Make a class patchwork quilt by sewing everyone's prints together.
- Print another color using a different stencil on top of the first. (See examples, above.)
- Use a combination of stenciling and screen printing to build up a picture.

LINOLEUM CUTS

- **Suitable for older students due to use of sharp tools.**

Safety Notes

- Children must keep both hands behind the cutting tool at all times.
- Tools are sharp and cut hands easily.
- If linoleum is hard, hold it against the heater, sit on it, or place it in hot water for a few minutes. Take care as tools slip across a cold surface easily.

❶ Draw the picture with chalk onto the linoleum. Fill in the areas you want to be white (non-printed).

❷ Using a number two or three V-shaped cutter, cut along all your lines and edges of the shapes. Now use a number five U-shaped cutter to dig out all the white chalk areas leaving raised areas that will hold ink and create an image.

❸ Create textured areas by crossed lines, nicks, brick-like patterns, single fine lines together, overall gauges, etc.

❹ Make a print. (See page 34, teachers notes.)

Equipment

linoleum cutting tools—one handle per child plus a selection of cutters, linoleum squares (which can be cut into quarters by the teacher with a ruler and a sharp knife), wooden bench hooks to slip over the edge of the desk to prevent fingers being cut while holding linoleum in place.